ARNAUD C. MARTS

Man's Concern

FOR HIS FELLOW-MAN

Published on the occasion of the 35th Anniversary of the founding of Marts & Lundy Inc. and the 70th Anniversary of the origin of the efficient, short-term fund-raising campaign.

PRINTED IN THE UNITED STATES OF AMERICA, BY THE W. F. HUMPHREY PRESS INC., GENEVA, NEW YORK

LIBRARY OF CONGRESS CATALOG NUMBER
61-9105

ARNAUD C. MARTS

Man's Concern

FOR HIS FELLOW-MAN

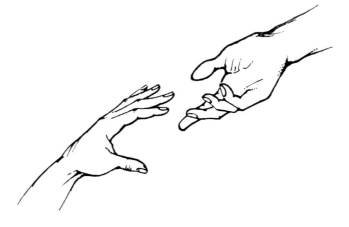

FOR HIS FELLOW-MAN

A Swift Review of Civilized Man's
Philanthropic Nature and Efforts

THROUGH FORTY CENTURIES
2000 B. C. —— 1961 A. D.

By ARNAUD C. MARTS
Chairman of the Board
Marts & Lundy, Incorporated

521 FIFTH AVENUE
NEW YORK 17, NEW YORK

1000 TWELFTH STREET, N.W.
CANTON 1, OHIO

Contents

ARNAUD C. MARTS

The author is now Chairman of the Board of Marts & Lundy, Incorporated, after serving as its president since the beginning of the organization. He is also a member of the boards of Oberlin College, from which he was graduated with Phi Beta Kappa honors, Wilkes College, Bradford Junior College, Woods Hole Oceanographic Institution and the American Leprosy Missions, Inc., of which he is Chairman. He is a former President of Bucknell University which he served for ten years on a two-day-a-week basis, after he had declined to leave his Marts & Lundy duties to accept the full time presidency. He had the unique experience of being requested by the students to accept the title as President of Bucknell after he had refused the invitation of the Trustees. A petition signed by each of the 1250 students was presented to him in a surprise session and a week later he capitulated. In 1941 and 1942 he also served in the cabinets of Governor James and Governor Martin as Executive Director of the Pennsylvania State Council of Defense, and in 1943–45 he was commissioned Captain in the U. S. Coast Guard Reserve, and appointed Chief of its wartime Temporary Reserve. He was co-founder in 1926 with George E. Lundy of the firm bearing their names, which in the 35 years of its service has raised over $1¼ billion in 1,979 campaigns for schools, hospitals, colleges, universities, churches, and other philanthropic institutions. He has been awarded honorary degrees by Hillsdale, Oberlin, Bucknell and Hobart. He is the author, among many brochures and articles, of the book entitled PHILANTHROPY'S ROLE IN CIVILIZATION, *(Harper & Bros. 1953) characterized as "a comprehensive and definitive treatise on the vast subject of American philanthropy and fund-raising."*

"This thing of giving," said George F. Burba, "I do not understand, any more than you do, but there is something about it that blesses us . . . Those who give most, have most left . . . I believe that everyone who dries a tear will be spared the shedding of a thousand tears . . . I believe that every sacrifice we make will so enrich us in the future that our regret will be that we did not enrich the sacrifice the more . . .

"Give—and somewhere, from out of the clouds, or from the sacred depths of human hearts, a melody divine will reach your ears, and gladden all your days upon the earth."

From: *"Philanthropy's Role in Civilization"*
BY ARNAUD C. MARTS

[8]

CHAPTER I

THE DAWN OF THE HUMANITARIAN SPIRIT
AND ITS MANIFESTATIONS UP TO
THE 20TH CENTURY

Mankind has taken long strides during the past forty centuries from the attitude of the average man of that era who naively inquired, "Shall I starve while my sister has children she could sell?"

There are probably hundreds of millions of people of our day who would be revolted if they should encounter a person with as selfish an attitude toward others. Rather, many of our generation respect and honor the man who feels an unselfish concern for the well-being of the less fortunate, and who demonstrates his desire to help his fellow men, indeed to help mankind as a whole to higher levels of civilized life. Succeeding generations have demonstrated this desire through private philanthropy and through political and social actions.

How and why have we made some progress in humanitarian good will? And how much progress have we made?

It is unfortunate that so few competent historians and scholars have turned their attention as yet to this aspect of the development of civilized man. Surely the very essence of civilization is the willingness of man to live in peace and good will with his fellow man. And strangely enough there have been thousands of books on wars and struggles and conflicts to less than one on good will and "love for mankind."

The historian who would help us to understand the slowly developing spark of human unselfishness from that cruel concept of our ancestor of forty centuries ago, quoted above, to the generosity of a typical citizen of America today who gives time and money and leadership to a dozen or more philanthropic agencies, would shed light on the very spirit and nature of civilized man.

[9]

Within only the past few years has there been any evidence of a scholarly interest in philanthropy, "the love for mankind", as a vital force in civilized society. In 1958 a dozen historians were invited by the Russell Sage Foundation to a conference at Princeton on The History of Philanthropy in the United States. This conference was convened by Mr. F. Emerson Andrews, consultant to that Foundation and the widely respected author on philanthropic foundations and philanthropy. These historians and specialists recognized "the inadequacy of historical research into philanthropy" and drew up a list of about 100 "suggested studies."

The Ford Foundation has made a grant which will finance a study of the history of American philanthropy under the direction of Professor Merle Curti, of the University of Wisconsin. Professor Irwin Wyllie is writing a book on the ideology of American philanthropy, and Professor Scott M. Cutlip, both of the Wisconsin faculty, is working on a history of organized fund-raising, both parts of the same project. Professor Robert Bremner of Ohio State University has written and published, also a part of this project, *American Philanthropy*.

Last year the Russell Sage Foundation published a valuable volume *Philanthropy in England 1480–1660,* by Dr. W. K. Jordan of Harvard University. As a result of these and other contemporary efforts of historians and scholars to trace the creation and development of man's concern for man over the centuries, undoubtedly the next generation will have a much better understanding of the spiritual nature of modern man.

But we of our generation are required to grope and dig and speculate as to how man's "love for mankind" developed over the centuries.

It took me, a rank amateur, for illustration, 30 years of reading and observation and experience to realize that philanthropy has been one of the noblest impulses which have stirred the hearts of fine-grained men and women of the past 4000 years. I propose in this brief panorama of *Man's Concern for His Fellow Man* to try to encourage others to realize that this unselfish spirit has deep roots in human history, and has within it the very essence of civilized and cultural progress.

I will review 3940 years of the philanthropic spirit very sketchily, and will soon get you into the 1890's when philanthropy, as we

GEORGE E. LUNDY

George E. Lundy, Honorary Chairman of the Board of Marts & Lundy, Inc. was born in Iowa and has been actively engaged in fund raising pursuits for over forty years. During World War I, his fund-raising ability was recognized by the various national funds that were being raised for war purposes and he was appointed director for Eastern Ohio of all the war work funds of that period. His success in this field brought him into national prominence, and he was sought in the post-war years by many organizations desiring the services of a skilled campaign director. He has since given his entire time to public relations and fund-raising for religious, educational, and philanthropic organizations.

His address, on the subject "Raising Money for Church Purposes" to the twenty-eighth annual Ohio Pastors Convention contained such good advice to churches that over 50,000 reprints of his address have been requested by pastors for distribution to their church officials. He has also authored several articles for religious magazines. He resides in Canton, Ohio.

LOUIS W. ROBEY

Honorary Vice-Chairman of the Board of Directors of Marts & Lundy, Inc., has been a member of this fund-raising organization for more than twenty-five years and has a wide and varied background in all phases of public relations and fund-raising. He is the author of many articles and handbooks on the subject.

Dr. Robey graduated summa cum laude, Phi Beta Kappa, from Bucknell University and with honors from the University of Pennsylvania Law School. He also holds an honorary degree of LL.D. from Bucknell University. He first practiced law in the office of the Hon. George Wharton Pepper in Philadelphia. In addition to his successful career as a lawyer, he has taught at Bucknell University, the University of Pennsylvania, and Temple University.

For many years he has served as Counsel on Public Relations and Fund-Raising for the American Baptist Board of Education. He is a member of Phi Beta Kappa, Order of the Coif, Phi Delta Phi, and Delta Upsilon, and is the author of "Outlines of Real Estate Law and Finance," "Check List of Fund-Raising Essentials," "Fund-Raising as a Profession," and "The Little More in Fund-Raising."

know it today, began to emerge into its present vast dimensions. And I will take you behind the scenes of modern philanthropic fund-raising, where you may see how the new profession of fund-raising counsel endeavors to assist the 40 century-long struggle for a better and nobler world.

ANCIENT SIGNS OF PHILANTHROPY

Although there is little concentrated material available for such a review, one may glean here and there hints and evidences and inferential references to the spirit and practice of philanthropy of early generations. As an example of the vacuum now existing in this area, the author of a best seller which paints the history of mankind in broad, swift strokes takes us through 150 pages of the story clear up to the third century A.D. before he once uses the word "charity." Even he, although consciously striving to interpret civilization in spiritual rather than military terms, ignored that quiet, unostentatious, yet persistent undertow—a developing sense of concern for the well-being of others—which has helped to draw humanity steadily onward toward a state of cooperative civilization.

One's search is rewarded however, if one persists, because instances and evidences of philanthropy jump unexpectedly out from the annals of even the earliest civilized life.

We find, for illustration, that the Hammurabic Code, written about 2000 B.C., adjured the Babylonian to take care that "justice be done to widows, orphans, and the poor."

As early as 1500 B.C. we find it recorded that the Phoenician gods demanded the first fruits of all products be given to the service of religion.

TITHE CONCEPT APPEARS

About 1300 B.C., Moses originated an effective technique of philanthropy—the tithe. The tenth part of the yield of the harvest had to be given to the Lord, in support of religion and for the relief of the poor. Every seventh year, the people were required to let their fields lie fallow and the poor were permitted to garner the spontaneous growth during that Sabbatical year. At every harvest a corner of each field was left unharvested for the poor. There are those who feel that the tithe technique has not been improved upon and who earnestly urge a renewal of the practice.

The Pentateuch commanded charity for the unfortunate members of society and insisted that benevolence was an imperative duty, not a matter of graceful choice. All through the history of the Jewish race righteousness has found its most practical and fervid expression in charity. "The Cell of Silence" or "Chamber of Whispers" was a later Jewish charity technique which came very near to being the ideal exercise of charity. These names were given to a quiet room in the synagogue into which the philanthropic entered unobserved, and left donations for respectable poor, who also entered unobserved to obtain the help they needed.

About 450 B.C., the gentle Gautama—Buddha to us—established in India a religion based upon self-restraint and charity for the poor. Two hundred years later we come upon the story of the first endowment of foreign missions. The good King Asoka was so impressed by the power of Gautama's simple code that he forsook and forswore war and conquest and greed, and devoted his money and his influence to spreading the Gospel as he understood it. He sent missionaries into all parts of the civilized world, even to Persia and Greece and Rome. He gave millions to endow Buddha's religion, and the consequences which have flowed from that piece of philanthropy are simply incalculable. Buddhism numbers 500 million adherents today in Ceylon, China, Japan, Burma, Siam, Kashmir and Tibet, although it has died out in India, the land of its birth.

Like all organized religions, it has become a vastly different thing from the original concept of its gentle founder. Our Western minds might question whether or not the net effect of Buddhism on the billions of human beings who have been its followers in the 2000 years since Asoka financed its early missionary outreach has been for good or evil. But we could not evaluate that without knowing what moral and religious patterns these people would have followed had there been no Buddhism. Certainly it was an immense improvement over the animism which it replaced.

One of the notable acts of philanthropy which we find was the gift of Alexander the Great in the fourth century B.C. to found Alexandria University in northern Egypt. It was a library, in reality, which became a veritable storehouse for the wisdom and art and skills of the past. Scholars came from all parts of the then western world to consult its manuscripts and to exchange knowledge. Until it was destroyed by fire set by the fleet of Augustus Caesar this monument to Alexander's philanthropy was the center of the culture of the Mediterranean world.

Alexander's philanthropy also financed Aristotle's Lyceum so generously that at one time Aristotle is said to have had a thousand men scattered throughout Asia, Egypt, and Greece, getting data for his Natural History.

CHRISTIAN AND JEWISH INFLUENCE

The Christian era marked the influx of new tides of unselfish regard for the welfare of humanity. At the very center of Jesus' teaching was the concept of one's responsibility for others. He exhorted his followers to "love thy neighbor as thyself," and he specifically prescribed charity to a certain rich young man as the very act of his salvation: "If thou wilt be perfect, go and sell that thou hast, and give to the poor."

Salamon Reinach, brilliant French critic, who views the progress of mankind rather coolly and certainly dispassionately, says that our whole western civilization has been influenced by four central ideas of the Jewish and Christian religions far more than by the philosophy of Greece or the teachings of Aristotle. Of these four ideas, which he calls "the foremost educative force in Europe," one is charity.

The Jews, since Christ, have also shown a sustained devotion to charity and philanthropy. They are no less generous than are the Christians of our nation. They have maintained their race-old tradition in this respect. Their great post-biblical seer and prophet Maimonides codified their charitable duties in 1204 A.D. in what he termed the Eight Degrees of Charity as follows:

> First, high degree, than which there is no higher, is that of one who takes hold of an Israelite who has become impoverished and gives him a gift or a loan or goes into partnership with him or finds work for him, in order to strengthen his hand so that he may be spared the necessity of appealing for help.
>
> Less than this (i.e. next below in rank) is the case of one who gives charity to the poor, without knowing to whom he gives and without the poor knowing from whom he takes.

[15]

Less than this is the case of the one who knows to whom he gives without the poor knowing from whom he receives. An example of this is the practice of distinguished wise men who used to go secretly and leave money at the doors of the poor.

Less than this is the case where the poor man knows from whom he takes but the giver does not know the receiver. An example of this is the practice of the wise who used to wrap up money in their cloaks and cast the bundles back of them (without looking), the poor coming afterward to pick them up, thus being spared all shame.

Less than this is the case of him who gives without being asked.

Less than this is the case of him who gives after he is asked.

Less than this is the case of him who gives less than is proper but in a pleasant manner.

Less than this is the case of him who gives reluctantly.

But let us pick up again the strand of philanthropy in the early Christian church, for it is that strand which leads directly to the far-flung effort of the present generation in America to advance the culture, the health, the character, the education and the well-being of humanity through hundreds of thousands of local, state and national voluntary associations and institutions which are maintained, not by law, nor by command, but by the free-will philanthropy of millions of men and women.

PHILANTHROPY A KEY TO CHRISTIAN STRENGTH

The love of mankind—philanthropy—seems to have been the key to the explanation of the strange strength of the Christian church of the first and second centuries. These people were utterly bewildering to the rulers and wise men of their day, as Ghandi was in his day, for they desired or coveted nothing for themselves. A Roman emperor said that one Christian missionary was worth more than a Roman legion in the penetration of barbaric Germany.

About 150 A.D., the Christians began to organize their charity work by creating in each church what they called a Church Fund. This was supported by voluntary gifts. Deacons dispensed funds to the needy.

Later districts or deaconries were organized. In each district was a hospital, an alms office, an orphanage, and a shelter for young babies. The hospital, or *Hotel Dieu,* was not a hospital in our sense, but a place of hospitality for strangers. As the centuries passed, however, modern hospitals grew out of these early *"Hotels Dieu."*

In 321 A.D., Constantine gave license to give or bequeath money to the church and from that time on enormous endowments began to accumulate around these Christian charitable institutions.

The church institutions, centers of good works, crude as they were, proved to be the lighthouses of civilization in those stormy centuries of cruelty and ignorance. "All through the darkest period of the Middle Ages," writes W. E. K. Lecky, in his *History of European Morals,* "through ferocity and fanaticism and brutality, we may trace the subduing influence of Catholic charity. Charitable habits, even when formed in the first instance from selfish motives, even when directed as to be positively injurious to the recipient, rarely fail to exercise a softening and purifying influence on character."

TWO NOBLE HERITAGES

Two of our noblest modern institutions evolved slowly from these charities—the hospital and the university. At first the hospital was a rest room or hospitalium in the house of the bishop, and Harnack states that the bishop himself was required to act as physician. The first documentary proof of a hospital is of one established at Caesarea in 369 A.D. by St. Basil. It was a veritable city, with pavilions for various diseases, residences for physicians, nurses, and convalescents. St. Gregory called it a "heaven on earth."

Following the Crusades, hospitals multiplied at an astonishing rate throughout all Europe and England. At one time there were attached to the churches and religious orders literally thousands of hospitals for lepers only. These were neither tax-founded nor tax-supported institutions. The revenue was derived chiefly from appropriations from the church, from private bequests and from endowments. The endowments of some hospitals grew so large that they owned farms, vineyards, houses and even whole villages.

The jousting tournament, Sir Walter Scott's description of which has thrilled every schoolboy who has read *Ivanhoe,* was often staged as a benefit for a medieval hospital. It might last a week or a fortnight, a carnival of sport which, like modern charity balls, would yield a financial return for the work of the humanitarian institutions. Various societies and guilds were established in aid of hospitals to which the people contributed membership fees. Thus, the early hospitals were created by those who *loved* mankind, not by those who *ruled* mankind.

During the bleakest night of the Dark Ages universities began to spring up at these centers of religion and charity and the dim embers of learning were fanned into flames again by men who had a "love of mankind." The early universities were not created by kings or rulers or by the rich. Indeed, the black gowns now worn by college seniors are said to have been worn originally to hide the rags in which the scholars were clad in medieval days. They were very modest institutions in the beginning and were looked down upon with scorn by the nobles. They were created by scholars of the middle class for the middle class and stand as a perfect illustration of how the people may work together in a voluntary philanthropic endeavor for the good of each and of all.

"VIVID AS A BEACON"

H. G. Wells, in summing up in his *Outline of History* the history and progress of the human race up to our day, pays this eloquent tribute to the "love for mankind" which we have been endeavoring to trace during the past four milleniums:

"It is only within the last three or at most four thousand years that we have any clear evidence that voluntary self-abandonment to some greater end, without fee or reward was an acceptable idea to men, or that anyone propounded it. Then we find spreading over the surface of human affairs, as patches of sunshine spread and pass over the hillsides on a windy day in spring, the idea that there is a happiness in self-devotion greater than any personal gratification or triumph, and a life of mankind different and greater and more important than the sum of all individual lives within it.

"We have seen that idea become vivid as a beacon, vivid as sunshine caught and reflected dazzlingly by some window in the landscape, in the teaching of Buddha, Lao Tse, and, most clearly of all, of Jesus of Nazareth. Through all its variations and corruptions Christianity has never completely lost the suggestion of a devotion to God's commonweal that makes the personal pomp of monarchs and rulers seem like the insolence of an over-dressed servant and the splendors and gratifications of wealth like the waste of robbers. No man living in a community which such a religion as Christianity or Islam has touched can be altogether a slave; there is an ineradicable quality to these religions that compels men to judge their masters and to realize their own responsibility for the world."

PHILANTHROPY CHANGES ENGLAND'S SOCIAL STRUCTURE

Dr. W. K. Jordan presents a striking historical illustration of how private philanthropy and political action brought about profound changes in every day life in English society in his book, *Philanthropy in England, 1480–1660,* recently published by the Russell Sage Foundation.

After a vast amount of research over a period of several years, Dr. Jordan is able to describe in detail the unprecedented generosity of merchants and bankers of that period. Their generosity was first directed toward the alleviation of poverty which was acute at that time for reasons which Dr. Jordan sets forth.

These generous merchants of London and of other large cities in England soon realized that alms alone could not cure the deepseated evils of poverty and they began to make still larger gifts to education. In that period they established and endowed numerous schools, and also founded and endowed colleges at the universities.

These generous philanthropists developed the charitable trust as the major instrument of their gifts and bequests. This instrument was encouraged and strengthened by political action in the Tudor and Stuart reigns. Perhaps the most important single political support for this up-thrust of private philanthropy was the Elizabethan statute of charitable uses.

Dr. Jordan sums up his account of "the surging flood of benefactions" of the merchants and gentry of London and England in the early years of the 17th century in this sentence: "They had, it is not too much to say, formed the shape of the modern world."

THE PHILANTHROPY OF OUR FOREFATHERS

This is a brief review of the development of man's concern for man down to early colonial life in America. Your attention is now directed to philanthropy in our western, or modern, society. I will mention the scope and techniques of American philanthropy up to the twentieth century, and will then tell of two young men who had a Multi-Billion Dollar Idea, which revolutionized American philanthropy.

Ever since 1620 A.D., when the Puritans landed at Plymouth, American settlers and succeeding generations have been determined to create and maintain in our nation the finest spiritual and educational and cultural agencies and influences which they could conceive. They presumably brought this philosophy with them in the first instance from England where they had seen wealthy men and women of the day literally change the nature of English society by their generous concern for their fellow man. They have plunged ahead with their own strength and resources to create schools, churches, colleges, hospitals, art museums, libraries, welfare agencies, and every other type of service to help make a better world.

The methods they used for 270 years up to the 1890's were simple, and home-made. The early history of Harvard tells of "a number of sheep bequeathed by one man; a pewter flagon worth 10 shillings by another; a half bushel of corn from another", all in response "to the loud groans of the sinking college."

Professor William E. Dodd describes the small beginnings of the mid-western colleges as follows:

"Peter Cartwright persuaded his people to contribute pitiful sums to the first Methodist College in Illinois; a shilling from one, a day's work from another, and a load of corn or boards from another."

BENJAMIN FRANKLIN, A LEADING FUND-RAISER

Fund-raising methods were improvised by resourceful men of each generation through the 17th, 18th and 19th centuries. Benjamin Franklin was one of the most successful and creative fund-raisers of that period. He would prepare a list of special prospects for each cause and then call personally upon each prospect. He raised funds to found a college (University of Pennsylvania), a hospital (Pennsylvania), America's first free library, a Presbyterian Church, a volunteer fire department and many other non-profit agencies and institutions.

Churches of the 1890's were using the oyster supper, the Sunday collection plate, cake sales, sociables, "poundings" or "showers"

AUSTIN V. McCLAIN →

President of Marts & Lundy, Inc. He is a graduate of Mercersburg Academy and of Washington & Jefferson College, where he served a number of years as Alumni Secretary and Development Director. He serves on the official boards of two secondary schools, as vice president of the Board of Regents of Mercersburg Academy, and as a member of the Board of Trustees of Moravian Seminary for Girls, Green Pond, Bethlehem, Pa. He is an elder of the United Presbyterian Church.

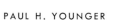

← PAUL H. YOUNGER

Executive Vice-President and Treasurer of Marts & Lundy, Inc. A graduate of Allegheny College, he served that institution as Assistant to the President and Director of Admissions, before joining the firm with which he has been associated for many years. At the present time he is a member of the Board of Trustees of Allegheny and of the Institute for College and University Administrators and the Methodist Church of Eastham. He is especially well known for his work in the area of corporation and foundation philanthropy. Among the many campaigns to which he has given direction was the multi-million dollar capital fund campaign of the United Negro Colleges.

THOMAS F. MORGAN, JR. →

Past President of Marts & Lundy, Inc.—1956 to 1961, and now Senior Consultant. Mr. Morgan has been associated with the firm since its inception in 1926. He has developed many new techniques of organization and has come to be regarded as one of the country's most versatile and successful fund-raising consultants. He is a Trustee of Wilkes College and is National Treasurer of the Lambda Chi Alpha fraternity. He is also a director of the John E. Mason Foundation, an agency created to aid young men planning careers in government service.

MELVIN D. BREWER

Vice-President and Secretary of Marts & Lundy, Inc. A graduate of Washington & Jefferson College, he served that institution as Alumni Secretary and Director of Admissions early in his career. He has directed outstanding campaigns for many leading colleges and universities.

HERBERT C. RICHMAN, JR.

Vice-President of Marts & Lundy, Inc. He was educated at Rutgers University and the University of Pennsylvania. The many programs to which he has given direction include the multi-million dollar Christian Higher Education Challenge of the American Baptist Convention.

JAMES H. DUCHINE

Vice-President of Marts & Lundy, Inc. A graduate of Bucknell University, he has handled the direction of many capital fund programs, especially among educational institutions.

(donations of food for the preachers' families), and home mission-ary barrels.

Colleges were using the "financial agent," frequently the president himself, who was sent to the eastern cities to preach in the churches and gather funds for the colleges of the west and south. Presbyterian financial agents went to New York and Pittsburgh; Congregationalists to New England; Methodists to New York and Philadelphia.

In the 1830's Miss Mary Lyon set out to raise $30,000 which she felt was necessary to launch a college for women which she had in mind. She traveled hundreds of miles in eastern states, visited 90 different communities and obtained 1800 subscriptions most of them ranging from 6 cents to $1 in size, and totaling $27,000. Thus began Mt. Holyoke College.

These fund-raising visitations to eastern cities by the financial agents of our 19th century colleges followed the pattern of our Colonial colleges, which had sent their agents *eastward* also—across the Atlantic Ocean to England and Scotland. Harvard, Yale, and Dartmouth, and others regularly sent fund-raising presidents or agents to England searching for donors. Yale found Elihu Yale; Dartmouth found Lord Dartmouth; Princeton sent Dr. John Witherspoon to Scotland and to the West Indies to raise needed funds. Planters of Virginia raised a travel fund to send Dr. James Blair to London, where he obtained gifts from King William and Queen Mary to found a college in Virginia. Its name became, of course, William & Mary.

THE PERSONAL APPROACH

This personal search for gifts was the major technique used all through the 19th century for founding and maintaining our colleges. Indeed, it was the accepted technique for college fund-raising in America right up to the close of World War I, when colleges began to use the Multi-Billion Dollar Idea created in the 1890's by the two young men whom I shall name on the following pages. I well remember that in the early 1920's one might still see at any given time, a half dozen or more college presidents at the Prince George Hotel in New York City, each in New York to search for funds for his college.

One recalls some of the great college presidents of the last 300 years, enthusiastic and dedicated fund-raisers, when one hears the cry of pain by a college president of our day who suddenly discovers that presidential duties include fund-raising.

"BEGGING" LETTERS

Hospitals, orphanages, and welfare agencies were using "begging" letters and are still using them. This method had been imported from London where the abuse of the technique became a contributing factor in the creation of the great Charity Organization Society which initiated our modern social agencies. Lists were for sale or rent with symbols after each name indicating the probable results to be obtained: — meant "doubtful"; X "Good"; G "will give again."

To the inexperienced it might seem highly profitable to acquire $10 by using a postage stamp to ask for it; but thousands of new names must be put through the mailing hopper to produce a few score interested and generous friends. It generally costs a philanthropic organization more than a dollar to raise the first dollar by mail from a new contributor. Later, if the contributor renews his first gift from year to year, the method of "begging" letters becomes more profitable. It is the line of least resistance to which certain organizations turn most readily. It would be interesting to know how many such letters are mailed in one year; the aggregate is enormous.

BENEFITS, BINGO AND CHARITY

Volunteer fire departments and community-improvement societies used carnivals, street fairs, lotteries, benefit performances, etc. Some of these were joyous social affairs, but the amounts raised for charity were tiny in proportion to the efforts. One exclusive charity ball in New York City is said to have raised not more than the cost of the gowns purchased for the occasion.

Games of chance and gambling have been strongly urged as "inexpensive" ways of raising funds. But, "all is not gold that glitters."

A recent report by the State Lottery Control Commission of New York State gave the figures on the operation of bingo games from the time the game became legal in New York State on January 1, 1958, to September 30, 1960. During that period the players paid $62,743,515 to the sponsoring organizations (charitable) and received back $44,-519,345 in prizes.

The organizations thus had a net profit of $14,289,648. It would appear that bingo provided charity only 23¢ from each dollar expended.

CHAPTER II

A MULTI-BILLION DOLLAR IDEA FOR
AMERICAN PHILANTHROPY

In the early 1890's two devoted young men did some creative work which provided the foundation for the nearly 8 billion dollar philanthropic annual giving of our nation in 1960.

Have you ever wondered how and why the generosity of Americans to our private, non-profit, public-service agencies suddenly shot up to unprecedented levels shortly after the turn of the twentieth century? Is it because we are larger in population? Is it because we are wealthier? In part, yes. But giving in America has increased far more in the twentieth century than has our population.

We gave a total of about $7,800,000,000 in 1959 to our religious, educational, health, social service, character-building and cultural agencies, according to the American Association of Fund-Raising Counsel.

Today's generosity is at the rate of $43.96 for each man, woman and child in America.

In 1910, when Mr. Lundy and I were getting our first experiences with organized fund-raising, the Amercian people gave a total of $536,000,000 to all philanthropic agencies. The per capita giving then was $5.82.

It is very interesting and quite revealing to compare the extent and depth of American generosity to our non-profit institutions with our business expenditures and investments. For illustration:

Our 1959 gifts of $7,800,000,000 were $137,000,000 more than all the money we spent in 1959 in all the stores of Woolworth, Sears Roebuck, Montgomery Ward, S. S. Kresge, Grand Union, and W. T. Grant combined.

In the fifty year period, 1910–1959, the American people gave to their philanthropic agencies $123,970,000,000. This is $15 billion *more* than the total accumulated invested capital of America's 500 largest industrial corporations, combined.

It is $40 billion *more* than the combined deposits of the 50 largest banks in America.

The total valuation of the property and endowments of our religious and educational and welfare agencies is $48,000,000,000. This is $1,781,140,000 more than the invested capital of our 50 largest railroads and airlines, and 50 largest utilities combined.

"SPECTACULAR" SUCCESS

Why has the growth of our generosity out-paced our growth in size in the twentieth century? One extremely important answer to this interesting question is found in the fund-raising methods which were created about 70 years ago by two young men recently out of college, Lyman L. Pierce and Charles S. Ward. Both are deceased. I had the privilege of knowing and working with each of them. May I tell you how they came to create this modern technique for stimulating the minds and hearts of Americans to increased philanthropic generosity?

These men were both young secretaries in the Young Men's Christian Association. Lyman L. Pierce, after graduating from the University of Minnesota in 1892, went into Y.M.C.A. work. An early job was financial and membership secretary at Omaha, Nebraska. Being a young man of superior ideals, spiritual capabilities, and courageous initiative, he was disturbed because his time was being devoted almost entirely to financial efforts necessary to keep the work alive. Far from accepting the situation, he began to work out a plan by which he could compress his membership and fund-raising tasks into a brief space of time and thus free himself during the remainder of the year for character-building work among the young men of the community.

Pierce enlisted 100 of the leading men of Omaha in a Y.M.C.A. membership campaign—each man to get one new member a month, until the total membership should reach 1500. These 100 men were divided into 20 teams. Printed matter was prepared and regular report meetings held. It was a great success—and lots of fun as well. News of the new method spread quickly throughout the entire Y.M.C.A.

CHARLES S. WARD (1858–1929)

Creator in the 1890's of the intensive fund-raising methods which came to be known as the "Ward Plan." Following spectacular success in fund-raising as the General Secretary of the Y.M.C.A. at Grand Rapids, Michigan, 1890–1897, he became the Financial Secretary of the International Committee of the Y.M.C.A. Both Mr. Ward and Mr. Pierce won additional national recognition of their methods during the record-breaking country-wide campaigns for World War I war work.

LYMAN L. PIERCE (1868–1940)

Co-founder with Charles S. Ward of the techniques of the intensive fund-raising program which has caused an incalculable up-surge in American philanthropy during the last 60 years. It was while he was Financial and Membership Secretary of the Omaha, Nebraska, Y.M.C.A. in 1893 that he first created fund-raising methods which became an important part of the "Ward Plan." He and Mr. Ward joined in the direction of an intensive fund-raising campaign at the nation's capital in 1905.

Charles S. Ward also entered the employ of the Y.M.C.A. when he was graduated from Dartmouth in 1881. In 1890 he became general secretary at Grand Rapids, Mich. He persuaded his directors to agree to close down their desks for a month and see a set number of people each day for subscriptions for the work of the Y.M.C.A. He promised that if they would do this, nothing more would need to be said or done about finances the rest of the year.

The newspapers told of this novel undertaking—"spectacular" it was termed in those days—and the whole city watched with intense interest. The eleven-month recess from financial solicitation proved a happy experience. It also proved so interesting to the rest of the Association brotherhood that Mr. Ward was called in 1897 to New York as financial secretary of the International Committee of the Y.M.C.A. He was invited to city after city to tell other local Associations of his experience at Grand Rapids and to help them put similar campaigns into operation.

Meanwhile, in 1900 Lyman Pierce had been appointed to the general secretaryship of the Y.M.C.A. in Washington, D. C. With his restless energy he brought about an extension of the program and gradually persuaded his directors to undertake to erect a new building to cost the unprecedented sum of $300,000. President Theodore Roosevelt gave strong backing. In 1905 Pierce requested the International Committee for the help of Ward in directing the $300,000 campaign in Washington. Here the paths of the two men met. Merging their ideas and experiences, they evolved the modern "whirlwind" campaign. It was Pierce who made the bold suggestion that the campaign be cut down from a month's to a week's time and that, in order to accomplish this result, a larger number of volunteer solicitors be enlisted. It worked!

THE PIERCE-WARD PROCEDURE

Following the Washington experience Ward adopted the "one week" plan as his standard practice. From that time on he directed similar Y.M.C.A. building campaigns in scores of cities. So widespread were his campaigns that they came to be known as the "Ward" plan. The greatest of these early efforts occurred in New York City in 1913, when the Y.M.C.A. and the Y.W.C.A. jointly determined to raise $4 million for needed new buildings. This announcement took New York's breath away. No single event in the field of philanthropy had ever been of so spectacular a nature as that unbelievable proposal to raise $4 million in a few days. But the campaign was a success. A total of $4,095,000 was contributed by 17,400 people. Four hundred of the contributors—including the John D. Rockefellers, father and son—gave $3,500,000 in large amounts, while 17,000 others followed their lead with smaller contributions totaling $495,000.

This and other similar achievements of the campaign method now began to attract the attention of hospitals, colleges and various welfare societies. Charles Ward was in great demand, and almost everywhere he went an amazing success resulted.

Lyman Pierce later spent a year traveling over the United States as field secretary of the Layman's Missionary Movement, and gave instruction and inspiration to laymen in the Protestant churches in the new technique of raising philanthropic funds. The intensive campaign method was adopted by many churches in what was called the Every-Member Canvass and, as a consequence, giving to Protestant churches experienced a sharp rise, which has continued to this day.

THE PLAN WIDELY ADOPTED

It was in 1914 that the first college I know of used the new campaign method effectively as a means of raising capital funds. This was the University of Pittsburgh then in transition from the old Western University of Pennsylvania, whose campus was being moved from Allegheny to the Schenley Park region. Charles Ward was lent by the National Council of the Y.M.C.A. to direct the campaign. By coincidence, Lyman Pierce was then general secretary of the Pittsburgh Y.M.C.A. and he participated as a volunteer worker in this successful campaign. And I, just out of college on my first job, was boys' work secretary on Lyman Pierce's staff, so I saw this college campaign in operation.

These two men, Pierce and Ward, were brought into national prominence in 1916–17 when Ward was drafted by Henry P. Davison, wartime president of the American Red Cross, to use campaign methods in the direction of the first $100,000,000 campaign for the Red Cross. Ward took Pierce with him as his associate. They were startlingly successful. Other war funds quickly followed, Y.M.C.A. War Fund, War Camp Community Service,

Hoover Food Conservation, etc., under their expert guidance, and when World War I was over, all philanthropic leaders of America were excitedly aware of this marvelous new fund-raising technique which could achieve unprecedented results for public causes.

Literally hundreds of colleges began to use the campaign techniques. Similarly, thousands of hospitals and welfare and religious organizations adopted this new fund-raising method. The Community Chest idea had grown out of fund-raising experiences in World War I, and hundreds of community chests were established throughout America.

PIONEER COUNSELLING FIRM

There was another Y.M.C.A. secretary named Harvey J. Hill, a scrappy, temperamental little dynamo who was general secretary of the Y.M.C.A. of Johnstown, Pa. when Pierce was in Pittsburgh. He went on to the Red Cross and other World War I campaigns with Pierce and Ward, and late in 1918 it was he who saw that if Ward and Pierce would set themselves up as a fund-raising firm after the war they would be sought by scores of hospitals, colleges and other non-profit institutions. Mr. Ward demurred because he was due back at the International Y.M.C.A. as soon as the war ended. We had numerous huddles on the 40th floor of the Metropolitan Tower where Hill was helping Harry Blair and me direct the National Campaign for War Camp Community Service. Frequently Hill talked about his ideas for such a fund-raising firm, and dictated memos about it far into the night.

Finally, Hill prevailed upon Ward to head such a firm and a partnership was formed in 1919—Ward, Hill, Pierce & Wells—with three other junior partners—the late Christian H. Dreshman, Olaf Gates, and myself. Mr. Dreshman became the head of the firm upon Mr. Ward's death in 1929. Herman Reinhardt is the present able head of this firm which is now named Ward, Dreshman and Reinhardt.

The top member of the first staff of the new firm was George E. Lundy of Canton, Ohio, who had participated actively in many war campaigns while on leave of absence from his duties as general secretary of the Canton Y.M.C.A.

Other members of the original staff were George Tamblyn, who formed the firm of Tamblyn & Brown; Bayard Hedrick who,

[31]

with Lyman Pierce, founded Pierce, Hedrick & Sherwood; and Howard Beaver, founder of Beaver Associates. Three years later, in 1922, T. F. Morgan, Jr. joined our staff. He is now Senior Consultant of Marts & Lundy, Incorporated. In 1926 George Lundy and I decided to form our own firm.

These original members of the various firms were committed to high ethical standards and practices as they pioneered in our new profession. We are proud of the efforts so many of them made to establish fund-raising as a useful and dignified profession rather than a competitive scramble for business and profits.

Louis W. Robey, honorary Vice Chairman of the Board; George E. Lundy, Honorary Chairman, and Arnaud C. Marts, Chairman of the Board of Marts and Lundy. These three have been responsible for the fund raising techniques which have raised over 1¼ billion dollars for philanthropy.

STATISTICAL MATERIAL

Mr. Lundy with the bound copies of the reports of Marts and Lundy Staff Conferences and the articles, booklets, and reports which have been prepared by members of the staff. This is one of the best sources of fund raising materials extant. Below, each file box represents the survey material and final report for each of nearly 2,000 campaigns. This is an important source for statistical material on which to plan campaigns of various types.

CHAPTER III

FORTY YEARS OF PROGRESS TOWARD PROFESSIONAL, VERSUS COMMERCIAL, FUND-RAISING FOR PHILANTHROPY

In the previous chapter I have told the story of how Pierce and Ward created a new fund-raising technique for philanthropy, a technique which has been used in the twentieth century to lift the annual giving in America from less than the $500 million level to the present level of nearly $8 billion. I have also noted briefly how, after World War I, the demand for expert technicians who were experienced in the use of this fund-raising device resulted in a new calling—that of professional fund-raising counsel. One hundred or more fund-raising firms are now operating in this field.

In this chapter I will trace the efforts of the firm with which I am most familiar, Marts & Lundy, Incorporated, to channel fund-raising counselling into professional rather than commercial patterns.

DIGNITY AND RESPECT PREFERRED

From our first days in full-time fund-raising careers in 1919, George Lundy and I were devoted to the goal of making our fund-raising more dignified and worthy of greater respect. At that time it was almost a reproach to be called a "professional money raiser." The public image of a fund-raiser (insofar as there was any recognition at all of the existence of such a practitioner) was that of a shallow, high-pressure slicker who had no interest in raising funds for philanthropic causes except for what he himself got out of it. "You've got a good racket" was not an unusual comment about our livelihood.

A certain hospital fund-raiser around 1915 was a flashy, spectacular, flamboyant person who had worked under Mr. Ward in one or two campaigns, and had then gone into fund-raising on his own as a free-lancer. However, instead of the quiet behind-the-scenes counselling position which Mr. Ward and Mr. Pierce always assumed, he took personal charge with fireworks and ballyhoo. The newspapers of a typical city would herald his arrival to put on a fund-raising campaign for the local hospital with bold headlines. Shortly after, they carried pictures of our hero leading a great civic parade to advertise the campaign. The parade had the usual components of floats, bands, pretty girls, and marching units but the main feature was the resplendent figure of our hero, the fund-raiser, dressed in frock coat and silk topper, standing erect on a float in the imposing posture of a circus ring master.

A life work with such a figure as its public image was repulsive to George Lundy and me, and to others who came into fund-raising careers as disciples of the Pierce-Ward methods. One of the basic instructions in the Pierce-Ward "school" of fund-raising was for the campaign director to stay in the background and bring to the volunteer business and professional leaders of the campaign his technical skill, guidance, and energy, unobserved by the public. As a result, many a campaign chairman has been praised publicly and effusively for miraculous results, at least one-half of which were due to the out-of-sight professional counsellor.

This is as it should be. Lyman Pierce used to say to me and others of his young trainees: "Remember the spirit of John the Baptist, the fore-runner of Our Lord, who said of his relationship to Jesus: 'He shall increase; I shall decrease.' This is your relationship to your campaign chairman, to help him be a successful leader of the campaign, not to grab credit and limelight for yourself."

MARTS & LUNDY, INCORPORATED, BEGINS

I shall not in this account tell in detail the story of the successes and the failures and the vicissitudes of our young firm. It started in 1926 very modestly, but quite auspiciously, with one account. This was the Presbyterian Pension Fund for $15 million led by the Honorable Will H. Hays as chairman, and the Honorable Andrew W. Mellon as treasurer. At the start we had a staff of six, including T. F. Morgan, Jr., president of Marts & Lundy, 1956–1961, and Paul A. Hightower, our number one surveyor. These are the only two men of that first staff who are still active in our firm. In

1931 Dr. Louis W. Robey, a lawyer of Philadelphia and long-time trustee of Bucknell University, joined us and soon became a full partner, serving for over twenty-five years as vice-president. He now is honorary vice-chairman and senior consultant.

I will take no more space to tell the story of this firm from its beginning except to say that over the years Marts & Lundy, Incorporated, grew in size to a permanent full-time staff of 55 well-trained men; that the number of campaigns we direct each year is now more than one hundred; that our gross income each year has grown from five figures to seven figures, and that, in the interim, we have managed more than 1900 campaigns for colleges, schools, churches, hospitals, and other non-profit institutions, raising nearly $1¼ billion.

But now to the main purpose of this chapter; to sketch briefly some of the measures Mr. Lundy and I and our associates have taken over the years in our endeavor to make fund-raising a dignified and respected profession rather than a commercial business.

PROFESSIONAL MOTIVATION

We chose this goal of a professional firm, rather than a commercial firm, for two basic reasons: primarily, because that was in line with our own life purposes, nurtured by our homes, our education, and our preference for lives of usefulness, our Christian philosophy of "The Fatherhood of God, and the brotherhood of man." Also, we had a conviction that the voluntary efforts of citizens of America to give their money and efforts to establish institutions of education, religion, health, character-building, and community service, constitute one of the noblest manifestations of American self-government. We were proud of the chance to work with such public-spirited citizens, and instinctively felt it was not fair to charge big fees just because the demand for expert fund-raisers was greater than the supply.

Don't misunderstand me. We needed income for our families and we were well paid, but not exorbitantly. We did not make money our personal goals. Rather, we aimed to do a good job. Like Ralph Waldo Emerson's maker of a better mouse trap, plenty of persons saw our work and liked it. Therefore, we were able to prosper while doing our best to bring our newly created fund-raising calling up to higher levels of professional status.

[37]

Some of the significant steps we have taken over the years in leading fund-raising toward professional rather than commercial standing are related on the following pages. There is no claim that professional status has been completely achieved, but we have tried and will continue to try, just as some others are doing. Fund-raising counselling is now an essential function in modern society and the nearer it approaches professional status the greater service it will render American philanthropy, and the greater will be the personal satisfactions and prestige of its practitioners.

I shall mention nine major categories of measures we have taken over the years to strengthen the service of fund-raising to American philanthropy:

1. Selection of staff
2. Selection by clients
3. Fees on a standard professional basis
4. Technical training of staff
5. Creation of guidelines based on analyses of past experiences
6. Creation of fund-raising programs based upon thorough surveys "in depth"
7. Publications
8. Creation of new fund-raising methods
9. Active support for philanthropic, educational, and religious agencies

As briefly as possible, the highlights of our efforts in these nine categories of our progress toward professional status are:

1. SELECTION OF STAFF

One very effective means which we used in creating a professional, rather than a commercial fund-raising firm, was to attract to our staff men whose life careers were already being guided by service motivations. We drew many of these men from positions which they had followed in religious and educational fields because of their basic desire to render service to their fellow men. It was not necessary for us to inculcate professional attitudes in these men. They came to us with such attitudes already a vital part of their lives.

Since the beginning of our firm we have had on our staff three college presidents, nine other college administrative officers, six clergymen, about 30 Y.M.C.A. secretaries. Thus was added great support to our desire to lead our fund-raising firm into ethical and professional channels.

2. SELECTION BY CLIENTS

We have been most fortunate in the institutions and their leaders who have selected us to counsel them in fund-raising. The vast majority of over 1900 philanthropic institutions which have been our clients have been led by men and women of great devotion and ability and we have been encouraged by them to work with them on a high plane of public service.

Our policy of never soliciting business has been an important factor in the professional character of our firm. The clients approach us in the first instance, and thus we are able to devote all our energies to serving our clients rather than to persuading them to retain us.

3. FEES

Out of nearly $1¼ billion which we have raised for our clients, we have never raised a dollar on a percentage or commission basis. Forty years ago I went to Nashville, Tenn., to direct a $35 million campaign for the Southern Methodist Church. We raised $53 million. I had barely returned to New York when a rumor spread throughout the whole south that I had been paid a fee of six percent. If this has been true I could have retired at that point with far more money than I will ever have. The truth is, I was paid $2000 a month for six months. I paid my own hotel and living expenses out of that salary.

We have been pressured time and time again by colleges, hospitals, and other philanthropic institutions to raise their funds on a contingent basis. We have never done so and never will.

In this connection, it might be well to explain how we compute our fees. The amount of money to be raised has no direct bearing upon our charges. Our fee is a service charge for the manpower needed. The base is a per month charge for a staff member whom we assign to give full time to the client. Multiply this per month charge by the number of months his services are required, and the result is our total charge, regardless of the amount to be raised. Our fee includes the part-time service of a staff writer who prepares copy and layout for the case book. It also includes the supervision and personal counselling of one of the officers of our firm. There are times when this fee formula has produced the same fee for each of two campaigns in operation at the same time in different parts of the country—one for $1 million and the other for $2 million—simply because the former campaign required more time to reach its scattered constituency.

Illustrations of the costs of various types of campaigns are interesting.

For a campaign, which produced over $15 million, the expense for publicity, travel, meetings, clerical work, *and* professional guidance was 5.4 cents per dollar raised. This is approximately the same amount any organization would have to pay to borrow a like sum for only a year, with the principal still to be repaid. The prospects were in every state of the nation, so the campaign required wide coverage.

A small college, nation-wide in alumni population, raised slightly less than $1,500,000. The total cost was 7.4 cents for each dollar raised.

A campaign for an independent school, which was confined to the immediate area, raised $1,100,000. The total cost was 3.3 cents per dollar raised, since less time was required for the campaign.

A hospital raised slightly under $1 million at a cost of 2.8 cents for each dollar.

These are typical situations, showing differences in costs, but also showing that the costs are not excessive.

A few years ago the New York State Legislature appointed a special committee to investigate fraudulent fund-raising for charity in this State, and I was requested by this committee to give public testimony as to the legitimate costs of fund-raising. I assembled considerable statistical data from a dozen large ethical fund-raising firms, and I testified that the total fund-raising costs of a properly conducted campaign vary from 3 percent in campaigns of over $1,000,000 to 17 percent in campaigns of $50,000—$100,000. I emphasized that the fund-raiser's fee was usually less than half of this cost. All of this fund-raising was done on a fee—not a percentage basis.

[40]

4. TRAINING OF STAFF

It is our practice to give all new staff members a thorough training in fund-raising techniques, regardless of how much previous experience they have had. Many have come to us from fund-raising positions in colleges and other philanthropic organizations. We put a completely inexperienced man in a training status for a period of time and pay him a salary while he learns the methods as an assistant to one of our resident directors. Later we may assign him as a field assistant in a large campaign supervised by an officer of the firm. We provide him with manuals, reference books (referred to in the following paragraphs) and give him personal coaching and guidance.

a. Annual Staff Conferences

All members of our staff are assembled each summer for instruction and for exchange of experiences during the past year. This summer training session was created by George Lundy and Louis Robey 15 years ago, and was planned and directed for 15 years by "Dean" Robey. It is the most comprehensive and effective fund-raising school of which I am aware.

All of the papers and discussions are published each year in a large volume. A cumulative index of all subjects discussed in these bound volumes is brought up-to-date each year by George Lundy. As a consequence, there is scarcely a problem which can come up in a campaign which a staff member cannot locate in our Cumulative Index with helpful comment.

b. Supervision by Officers

Back of our staff member, assigned as the resident director of a campaign, is one of the officers of the firm who is ready by personal visitation, mail, or phone, to confer and counsel and guide. Each of the six officers at headquarters has under his simultaneous supervision five to ten campaigns. Through him the firm can funnel out to the resident director all the firm's accumulated professional experience and talent in the service of the client.

5. CREATION OF GUIDELINES

A profession, or even a sub-profession, needs guidelines for its practitioners, based upon a mass of evidence culled out of past experience. This we have created under the leadership of George Lundy, our master statistician. In his files, he has accumulated a vast amount of evidence which he has assembled for ready use.

How much money will a church of 655 members who contribute $40,000 a year for current expenses be able to raise for a new educational building?

How much can a college with 18,000 alumni, situated in a city of 35,000 people, raise for a new library?

What is the per capita amount which a hospital can expect to raise from the constituency for a Nurse's Home?

What is the amount which any of these institutions should expect to pay in a fund-raising campaign for printing, meetings, postage, clerical help, etc.?

How much can an independent school expect to raise from the parents of students?

What part of the total goal of any campaign do the trustees usually give?

What percentage of the prospects will give if they are called on in person? By mail?

All of these guidelines, and scores of others, are available from the analyses which George Lundy has available.

PATTERN OF GIVING IN A CAPITAL CAMPAIGN

Frequently we encounter a devoted but inexperienced leader who believes that his institution can raise a large capital fund by persuading all of the friends of the institution to give equal amounts. For example, one such leader, before he consulted with us, had announced his plan to ask 500 friends to give $1000 each in order to raise $500,000. This is good arithmetic but very poor fund-raising.

As a matter of actual experience, about 80% of the total of a non-recurring capital fund for any given college, hospital or other philanthropic institution is almost always given in large amounts by 10 to 20 percent of the donors. One of the most widely useful guidelines created out of our past experience is a percentage table of the size of gifts needed to raise a large capital fund for a college, or hospital, or other community-supported institution. This percentage table was reduced to a formula by Dr. Robey in a $15 million campaign for Cornell University in 1950. It was based upon

[42]

ORGANIZED CONVOCATIONS

A well organized convocation attracts thousands of people and directs attention of thousands more to the work of a school or college. Above is part of the crowd at a recent Dartmouth College convocation on the theme: "Great Issues in the Anglo-Canadian-American Community." Former Ambassador Lewis W. Douglas was chairman.

actual experience in hundreds of capital fund campaigns and has become one of our important guidelines. It proves itself with almost unerring accuracy over and over again.

ANALYSIS OF TWENTY-YEAR FUND-RAISING ACHIEVEMENTS OF COLLEGES AND UNIVERSITIES

The late Dr. Philip King, our director of research, has created an analysis of the fund-raising achievements of all accredited colleges and universities in the past 20 years. Our files disclose whether your college stands in 10th place or 400th place in increase in assets, or in fund-raising results. His tabulation shows it—a unique contribution to our guidelines.

6. CREATION OF A FUND-RAISING PROGRAM BASED UPON A THOROUGH SURVEY "IN DEPTH"

When George Lundy and I started our fund-raising careers about 40 years ago, all we knew about a client to which we were sent to direct a campaign was the name and address of the president, if it was a college; or the chairman of the board, if it was a hospital. Our information and our planning started upon arrival. One of the important contributions we have made to fund-raising as a profession has been to require a thorough study of the institution's constituency, needs, and leadership before offering our services for actual fund-raising.

Fifteen years ago, while I was on a two-day-a-week leave of absence from Marts & Lundy to serve as president of Bucknell University, Messrs. Lundy, Robey, and King, created and copyrighted a *Survey Manual* which includes 30 printed forms on which to gather the facts essential to such a preliminary survey. The "depth" feature of this survey is the personal interviewing by our field surveyor of 50 to 100 supporters or potential supporters of the institution. The reports on these interviews enable us to "feel the pulse" of a cross section of the constituency as to its readiness to go into fund-raising, and, when not ready, to recommend measures which should be taken to bring it to a state of enthusiasm.

These field interviews were adopted after we were chided years ago by the late able president of Hendrix College in Arkansas, Dr. J. H. Reynolds. We had given him our opinion as to how much money we thought his college could raise in a campaign. He said:

[44]

MARTS AND LUNDY STAFF

The Staff of Marts and Lundy assembles once each year for a carefully planned period of review, when officers and staff members share their experiences and discuss the techniques growing out of nearly 2,000 campaigns.

"That's your opinion, but what do the *folks out yonder* think about it?" What he meant was:—what do the people who are going to be called upon to work and give think about us?

It was a pertinent question, and for many years we have made it our concern to go out into the field to find out what 50 to 100 selected "folks out yonder" think about the proposed campaign.

Based upon the information gathered on the 30 forms in our *Survey Manual,* and upon the attitudes of the persons interviewed, our officers then are able to express a professional opinion of how much can be raised, when, how and at what cost. These factors are carefully considered by the client and ourselves. If we then go forward with the campaign, our director goes to the client with a full blueprint of the program which is understood by both parties. It is, we believe, a long step toward responsible, competent professional performance.

During the last five years we have made 152 such fund-raising surveys for hospitals, colleges, schools and other philanthropic institutions.

As a result of our recommendations 111 of these clients moved into fund-raising campaigns which we directed. The other 41 were advised by us to postpone fund-raising until certain preliminary steps should be taken, or to use some other fund-raising methods.

The 111 clients for whom we planned and directed campaigns after our survey reports undertook to raise $115,463,188. They succeeded in raising $133,282,853.

We believe it is better for both the client and the firm that there be a modest fee for the survey, so that there is no obligation on either side to go ahead with a campaign. In other words, the fee provides the client with a professional opinion on what steps are necessary for a campaign and what the probable cost will be. We keep the price of the survey at less than actual cost, so that both parties share in the cost.

The professional objective character of these surveys is established by the fact that often we advise against the contemplated campaign, or against projecting the campaign until a year or more of activity in strengthening the weak factors discovered through our study. By this advice we discourage, or postpone, a contract. What could be more professional and less commercial!

A very important by-product of our "in depth" survey is the

opportunity it gives us to help the client understand in advance the nature of the service which a professional fund-raising firm provides. Many experienced leaders of philanthropic institutions already realize that they retain fund-raising counsel to train, teach and help them and their friends raise their own funds, not to solicit funds for them. But there are many inexperienced philanthropic leaders who do not know this, and consequently are shocked to discover that they can't "buy" fund-raising, as they buy an article in a store—"Wrap it, send it to my address, and mail me the bill." During the progress of one of our surveys we are able to explain in full just what the leaders of a school, a hospital, or other non-profit institution do in a fund-raising campaign, and just what the professional fund-raising firm does to earn its fee.

Before we created our "in depth" preliminary survey, we sometimes were blasted, in the midst of a campaign, by an irate leader whom we were urging to get into action, who would say: "I thought we hired *you* to do all this. You're making *me* do the work! What are we paying *you* for?" When such a leader calmed down, and did as he was advised, and the campaign succeeded, he would thank us for having been insistent, and would admit that no outside solicitors could have achieved the results.

7. NEW METHODS

While the basic principles—which call for an organization of volunteer, unpaid solicitors, concentrated effort and the assignment of responsibility for personal solicitation—are still in force, as Messrs. Ward and Pierce created and codified them nearly 70 years ago, it is essential to create new features to meet new fund-raising requirements as life in America becomes more complex. I shall mention only five in addition to those I have already described— the great convocation in advance of fund-raising, the regional organization in a nationwide program, our counselling service, our consultation meetings, and our "sales schools."

a. The Convocation

This is a public relations plan devised for the purpose of lifting a college, or a hospital, or other cause, up to public view and appreciation before the volunteer solicitors start out to call on the prospective contributors. It serves its purpose well, provided successful creative imagination is put into planning it. The Mid-

Century Convocation of M.I.T. at which the Hon. Winston Churchill was the featured speaker; the Case Institute Diamond Jubilee Convocation which headlined President Herbert Hoover; the Convocation at Transylvania College, at which President Dwight D. Eisenhower was the speaker; the One Hundredth Anniversary Convocation of Cooper Union at which Admiral Lewis Strauss was the honored guest; the New York University-Bellevue Medical Center Convocation, at which Gen. Alfred M. Gruenther was the main speaker; the Dartmouth College Convocation which featured the Prime Minister of Canada, the Hon. John G. Diefenbaker; and the Convocation at Brown University attended by 25,-000 on the theme of "Man's Contracting World in Our Expanding Universe", at which Ambassador Winthrop Aldrich presided, and in which a score of statesmen, diplomats, scientists, educators, and business leaders participated—each of the convocations gave great impetus to the major fund-raising campaign which followed, as did a score of similar convocations for other philanthropic institutions. We believe the creation of this device has helped to increase the dignity and worth of fund-raising, and has advanced fund-raising another step away from the ballyhoo status of our hero described previously, dressed as a circus ring master, and toward respected professional status.

b. The Regional Organization

Back in the 1920's when organized fund-raising was young, colleges began to use the radio in a campaign to hook up alumni all over the land in a simultaneous fund-raising opening dinner. When TV was invented, it was used for the same purpose. We discovered, while these were interesting and exciting publicity "stunts" they did not, alone, take the fund-raising appeal down into the checkbooks of the alumni. Consequently, we created the regional type of fund-raising organization, which called for a series of campaigns, in one region after another. Thus the appeal is brought directly to each potential subscriber by volunteer solicitors under the leadership of a local committee, rather than by way of the watered-down leadership of remote control.

c. Our Counselling Service

This is counselling service for certain clients whose officers are ready and willing to lead in a fund-raising program, but do not know the best technical methods to use. We can help some such clients, and are doing so. For illustration, the American Baptist Board of Publication and Education has retained the counselling services of our Dr. Robey for 19 consecutive years; Lehigh University has retained the counselling services of our Austin V. McClain for 15 years; and Franklin & Marshall College has retained his counselling services for 12 years.

d. Consultation Meeting

Another important new device which we have created is that of a consultation meeting prior to the public announcement of a fund-raising campaign. To this meeting 50 or so leading citizens of a community are invited to discuss informally the proposed program, and after a full discussion, to pass upon whether or not to have a campaign, and if so, how much the objective should be.

We first discovered the value of this technique in a small midwestern city where George Lundy was helping a college get into a major fund-raising program. A few years before, he had helped the college raise a few hundred thousand dollars. It had been a difficult campaign, for the reason that the college had made no effort to raise capital funds for 15 or 20 years.

Consequently the "giving muscles" of the community and of the alumni had grown flabby and weak. In the first small campaign the citizens of the community gave about $65,000. Now Mr. Lundy was back in the same city five or six years later to help the college raise a sum in seven figures. He knew if the campaign were to succeed it would be necessary for the local citizens themselves to give at least $500,000. He also knew that it would be a great shock to the citizens if the college should ask them for that unprecedented amount. He suggested, therefore, that the president request one of the leading citizens to invite a group of about fifty outstanding leaders of the city in a consultation dinner.

This was done, and at the dinner the president of the college first outlined his plans and dreams for the betterment of the college's educational services. From that point on, the men present took over the discussion as to how these plans could be implemented. Before the meeting was over these leaders had offered to undertake to raise $500,000 in the local city and the most influential leader in the community had consented to chair the campaign.

In due time, the whole half million was subscribed more enthusiastically than had been the $65,000 in the previous campaign.

This experience, and other similar experiences in other campaigns for hospitals, colleges and community institutions, led us to our present policy of making frequent use of such consultation meetings. The secret of the success of this device is that it transfers the responsibility for the success of a campaign from the institution which needs the money to the people who are going to give the money.

e. The Coaching Session or "Sales School"

In the early years we used to start off the general solicitation in a campaign with an inspirational dinner, to which all the volunteer workers or solicitors were invited. The following morning they started to visit their prospects. (In our campaigns no group solicitation is ever done at any campaign dinners; each prospect is visited privately and individually.)

But experience proved that inspiration alone did not suffice to prepare the volunteer worker to do effective and intelligent soliciting. So, about twenty years ago, we created the "coaching session" or "sales school" for the volunteer workers.

At this session we give the volunteers full information as to the purpose for which the money is being raised, and coach them carefully as to the proper and effective method of solicitation. At this session they select cards for the persons whom they are to visit and are given the opportunity to ask many questions as to the "why and how." We have prepared a motion picture film which has the "do's and don'ts" of soliciting, and inspiration for their public-spirited services to the philanthropic cause.

As a result many of them have become well informed and effective advocates of a great humanitarian cause, instead of rather bored and reluctant "drive" workers anxious to dispose of their pack of prospect cards as quickly as possible.

One of the reasons for the notable results in improved public relations which follow our campaigns may be traced to these "sales schools" which have prepared the voluntary workers for informative solicitation rather than for high pressure begging.

8. PUBLICATIONS

One of the essential elements in a dignified vocation or profession is the creation of thoughtful and informative literature on the subject. I believe the men of Marts & Lundy have produced more useful printed material in the general field of philanthropic fund-raising during the past 40 years than has come from any other one source. Most of these papers have been published in journals and magazines, and then have been reprinted by the thousands and distributed to the philanthropic field. Some were speeches which were later printed and distributed.

Appendix A on page 58 lists papers published and distributed to the philanthropic public by members of Marts & Lundy. More than 75,000 copies of *This Thing of Giving* were requested. Also, 50,000 copies of *Freedom to—America's Unique Freedom,* and over 60,000 copies of *Raising Money for Church Purposes* were requested.

In 1953 I used the notes and observations that I had been making for over 30 years to write a book called *Philanthropy's Role in Civilization.* This was published by Harper & Brothers and is regarded as one of the few published efforts to describe philanthropy and trace its development in civilized life. This book is on the shelves of over 600 college and public libraries in the United States.

In 1945–46 it was a privilege to finance for the American College Public Relations Association the publication of their first textbook on *College Public Relations,* written by W. Emerson Reck.

In 1955 we provided the funds to enable The American Foundations Information Service to bring out the seventh edition of *American Foundations and their Fields,* which remained the current directory of foundations until July 1960 when the Foundation Library Center published *The Foundation Directory Edition I* under the initiative of Mr. F. Emerson Andrews.

In 1959, after the death of Mr. Raymond Rich, the owner of this service, we assumed, at the request of his widow, Mrs. Wilmer Rich, his obligations to prepaid subscribers to his monthly news bulletin on *Foundations Information,* and we financed the publication of these bulletins to the end of the subscription period in June, 1960. We then transferred all of his extensive records on foundations into our permanent files.

9. PUBLIC RELATIONS SERVICES

Our development of the well planned campaign has caused us to suggest many public relations techniques for institutions. We use the expression "public relations" here in its correct sense, as contrasted with press agentry. Our public relations function has been recognized in statements by many institutions served by Marts & Lundy. Time after time we were told "The money you raised was important, but equally important was the great public relations result of the program."

As we observed it, the steps we were working out in our various campaigns were all directed at creating a better spirit toward our client, quite aside from their function as campaign tools. The survey itself, which seeks the opinions of 50 to 100 individuals, is an example. Other steps which add friends and disseminate information are: the consultation meeting, convocation, meetings of prospects, meetings of workers, campaign publications, regional meetings and the many other group affairs which bring to the service of our clients the most concentrated public relations programs most of them ever previously used.

The inexperienced person fears that a campaign will be a burden to the constituency, and odious to prospective subscribers. Exactly the opposite can prove true. A well conducted fund-raising campaign is the best public relations program possible to create new friends and warm the hearts of old friends.

10. SUPPORT FOR OTHER PHILANTHROPIC EFFORTS

I have spoken of our efforts within our own Marts & Lundy firm to move the fund-raising calling into professional, rather than commercial channels. Finally, I shall mention a few such efforts we have made outside our firm.

a. College Publicity Association

In the 1920's our publicity director, the late Mr. T. T. Frankenberg, founded the College Publicity Association. For 20 years this Association, which changed its name to its present one (American College Public Relations Association) grew steadily in size and influence, but had no permanent headquarters. Each year its address was that of its current president. In the mid-1940's their officers asked our advice as to the establishment of a permanent headquarters. We suggested they seek space in Washington with the Association of American Colleges. Dr. Guy Snavely, Executive Director of the latter Association, was agreeable in principle, but had no available space. He agreed to acquire the space if someone would pay the rent. We made a contribution toward the rent of this additional space for a few years until the A.C.P.R.A. was able to operate on its own resources.

b. Development Director

In the 1930's and 1940's I spoke several times before educational groups in advocacy of the creation of a development department in a college or university, and of the appointment of a full-time director of that department who would be as important an administrative officer as any of the other half dozen officers on the president's staff. These speeches were reprinted and distributed quite widely, and I believe this was an important factor in the movement of many colleges and hospitals to appoint such development directors.

c. "No More Large Gifts?"

Another general service was an article prepared in 1934 entitled "No More Large Gifts?", in which I challenged the statement by a famous university president which was being parroted by many other educational and religious leaders of that day, that "We have come to the end of large giving. In the future, all philanthropy must be supported by a multiplicity of small gifts." The article, for *School and Society*, was reprinted by the thousands, and it is said to have had a profound effect upon re-activating fund-raising following the depression of the 1930's.

d. American Association of Fund-Raising Counsel

In the early 1930's, it became apparent to leaders in the fund-raising field that this new technique for raising vast sums of money for philanthropic purposes might easily be captured by unscrupulous persons and used for selfish purposes. Consequently, the presidents of three firms, of which Marts & Lundy was one, invited representatives of a half dozen other firms to an informal conference to discuss the advisability of organizing an association of ethical fund-raising firms for the purpose of establishing and maintaining high ethical standards and practices. Out of this grew the American Association of Fund-Raising Counsel. The number of firms in this Association has grown to a present roll of 32.

I was honored to serve three terms. In my second term I worked with Senator Bernard Tompkins in his investigation of fund-raising frauds in New York state and gave public testimony in the Tompkins hearings as the representative of ethical fund-raising firms.

Following the Tompkins investigation and report my final effort as president of the Association was to establish a permanent office with a salaried secretariat in an endeavor to "help police fund-raising from within", in the words of Senator Tompkins. Prior to that year, the Association had not had its own headquarters or staff. It had functioned each year from the office of its current president, who was always the president of one of the member firms. Its program had been two dinner meetings a year at which officers of the member firms gathered to exchange experiences.

Marts & Lundy hoped that this Association would make a strong effort to direct ethical fund-raising into professional rather than commercial channels. It is too soon to know whether or not this hope will be realized. This Association could easily drift into the status of a trade group, unless a strong majority of the members should continue to insist upon the fulfillment of its original *ethical* and *professional* purposes.

In addition to these specific instances of services which we have rendered the wide field of American philanthropy, the officers and staff members of Marts & Lundy are called upon to serve as laymen in many posts of leadership in philanthropic institutions. Some are trustees of colleges, of schools, of hospitals. Others are officers in their churches, Boy Scout Councils, Y.M.C.A.'s and other religious and community agencies.

In short, though fund-raisers, they are no longer asked: "What is your racket?" On the contrary, they are accepted as useful citizens, engaged in a lifework of dignity and esteem. Their wives and children no longer find it embarrassing or difficult to explain their occupation.

At any rate, after 40 years of effort to bring fund-raising up to a higher level of professional status, we can feel that we have made some progress.

In this chapter I have briefly set forth some of the efforts our firm, Marts & Lundy, Incorporated, has made toward creating professional status for fund-raising counsel. Of course, other persons and other groups have also made their efforts. It is to be hoped they also will tell the story of their efforts, for much more literature on the subject is needed.

In the first chapter I endeavored to sketch briefly the development of civilized man's concern for his fellow man; and the impetus given to this development by the Judeo-Christian concept of the "brotherhood of man under the Fatherhood of God." I pointed out the flowering of this concept in America, where the private citizen has been encouraged to take the initiative in establishing and supporting, with his own gifts, non-profit agencies of service to society. I traced the "home-made" fund-raising methods used during the first 270 years of our life in America from 1620 to 1890. In the second chapter, I related how in the 1890's two young secretaries of the Young Men's Christian Association, Lyman Pierce and Charles Ward, dedicated to efforts to help make a better world, created new intensive and successful fund-raising methods which ushered in a vastly expanded era of cultural, educational, health, spiritual, character-building and community progress.

In the third chapter, I traced the creation and development during the past forty years of an entirely new "profession" or life-work, that of the "fund-raising counsel." I called attention to the phenomenal increase of giving by the American people to non-profit agencies as a result of the services of these fund-raising practitioners who learned to apply and to adapt the new methods which had been created in the 1890's by Messrs. Pierce and Ward.

I suggested that these practitioners would render a greater service to the welfare of mankind if they would seek to direct their fund-raising counselling into professional rather than commercial channels.

In conclusion, may I emphasize this suggestion?

During the forty years of my activity in this field, I have seen the giving public, in three separate decades, rebel against fund-raising in a rather general way. The first time was in the mid-1920's when hundreds of colleges took up the new "campaign" methods with a rush and all over the land began to pressure their alumni to "pay their debt to *alma mater*." Too little was said to the alumni about the greater and nobler service their alma mater could render mankind if she were supported more generously. And too much was said about the fact that alma mater had given them an education below cost and that they should now pay up. This worked well enough once, but when alma mater made a big point of the same debt a few years later in a second appeal to the same alumni, some cynicism and resentment resulted.

The second incipient revolt was observable in the late 1940's when irresponsible opportunists in various sections began to exploit the charitable impulses of the American people with fraudulent fund-raising schemes. I have previously referred to the investigation of charity frauds by the New York State Legislature. These practices were so flagrant that a wave of suspicion of all fund-raising swept over the nation, and several states passed laws in an endeavor to regulate and supervise fund-raising.

The third revolt, which I have observed, is one that began about two years ago against the multiplication of appeals that sprang up rather suddenly in behalf of numerous campaigns projected by committees formed to battle certain diseases. These new committees were sparked by the wide successes achieved by the National Foundation for Infantile Paralysis, the American Cancer Society, and the American Heart Association. Each of these organizations raised large sums to finance research in the causes and cures of these dreaded killers. As a consequence, about fifty national societies and their thousands of local chapters have since been created to raise funds for attacks on other named diseases.

Many of these "disease committees" tried to duplicate the fund-raising methods of the three pioneer societies, and the average good citizen has become callous and rebellious to the repetition of appeals.

If we trace the reasons for these three "givers" revolts, it seems quite apparent that they could have been prevented if all fund-raisers had operated on high standards of professional training and civic responsibility. Certainly some of the fund-raisers for these causes did serve with skill, but also certainly many did not.

The truly professional fund-raiser screens his clients carefully and counsels only those who, he believes, are endeavoring to render a useful service to mankind, and have a sensible and practical plan for so doing.

The truly professional fund-raiser serves only those clients who can justify in the public interest the fund-raising methods which will be involved in the fund-raising effort.

The truly professional fund-raiser will make sure that the appeal will be directed to the understanding and intelligence and the sympathetic heart of the giver in terms of "man's concern for mankind" and will not be geared to high pressure the giver into doing something which he really does not understand or want to do.

Such a truly professional fund-raiser will, eventually, be recognized as a force and power in civilized man's concern for his fellow man, and in his efforts to create a better world here on this earth. And giving in America, under such fund-raising leadership, will expand; and more givers will experience the inner satisfactions which come to the men and women who share voluntarily in an effort to heal the sick, to right an injustice, to protect a child, to comfort the afflicted, and to give a helping hand to a fellow man.

Man's concern for his fellow man, which began to make itself noticeable, feebly, forty centuries ago, has become one of the important criteria of modern civilized life, by which peoples judge and are judged.

It is now a force which must be reckoned with—in government, in politics, in business, in education, in all the institutions of modern society.

Private philanthropy continues to be the pioneer, the prod, the conscience, the standard bearer of many of mankind's endeavors to build a better world, in which we hope all men ultimately may live in peace and justice and freedom and mutual well-being.

America continues to be a world leader in the philanthropic efforts of our private citizens, and in the political efforts of our government to create a better society in those sections of the world where men need and wish our help in the efforts toward a better life.

It is to be hoped that the American giving public, those more than 30,000,000 private citizens who give generously each year to our philanthropic agencies, will always remain deeply conscious that their gifts are an essential force in man's forty centuries-long concern for his fellow man.

Sometimes we are annoyed by importunate appeals for gifts to this, that, or the other philanthropic agency; and sometimes we have a right to be annoyed. But, for the most part, when we do give in response to appeals made by agencies known to be worthy, we take our place "on the side of the angels" in mankind's endless aspirations for "the brotherhood of man and the Fatherhood of God."

Every such unselfish act, however small or large, adds a bit more weight on the side of goodwill as our civilization wavers on the edge of danger, seemingly too evenly balanced between brutality and goodwill. I hope and believe that the great majority of our "givers" will remember this, even when sometimes annoyed by unwelcome solicitations.

If they can remember it, they will get a well-deserved lift of spirit from the consciousness of being in the long succession of over 40 centuries of a growing number of fine-grained, unselfish men and women. May they feel invisible bonds with millions of others who believe, in those words of H. G. Wells previously quoted, "in a life of mankind different and greater and more important than the sum of all individual lives within it."

APPENDIX A

A Listing of Published Articles on Philanthropy written by members of the Staff of Marts & Lundy, Incorporated

BY ARNAUD C. MARTS

1929	A Campaign Director Looks at his Job	*The Survey*
1932	The Colleges in the Newspapers	*Association of American Colleges Bulletin*
1932	A 5 or 10 Year Financing Program for a College	*Association of American Colleges Bulletin*
1932	Two Ways to make a Mousetrap	*The Christian Century—and Readers Digest*
1932	Engineers or Mustard Seed?	*The Christian Century*
1933	Survival of the Fittest	*Literary Digest*
1933	The Stability of the Church	*Federal Council Bulletin*
1933	Financing Philanthropy over the Centuries	*Social Science*
1933	Are Scholars News?	*The American Scholar*
1934	The Campaign of Perseverance	*Association of American Colleges Bulletin*
1934	No More Large Gifts?	*School & Society*
1934	Are the Churches Insolvent?	*The Christian Century*
1934	College Football & College Endowment	*School & Society*
1934	Philanthropy under the New Deal	*The Christian Century*
1934	Developing the Fine Art of Giving	*Literary Digest*
1936	Men and Money	*American Bankers Association*
1936	Should Colleges Train Philanthropists?	*The Key Reporter*
1936	Saving Through Giving	*Bulletin of American Library Association*
1936	Advancement Voluntarily or by Statute?	*Social Science*
1937	Higher Education for Such a Time as This	*Christian Education*
1937	Education's Lost Team Mate	*Presbyterian Banner*
1938	30,000,000 Philanthropists	*The Key Reporter*
1938	Do Taxes Kill the Golden Goose?	*The American Scholar*
1940	The Lawyer's Place in the Community	*New Jersey Bar Association Year Book*
1940	Publicity and Public Relations Plans	*Association of College and University Business Officers*
1941	Do You Care?	*Watchman Examiner*
1941	The Real Purpose of Education	*The Intercollegiate*
1941	Challenge & Opportunity	*Think*
1942	Colleges & Universities in the War Effort	*Association of College and University Business Officers*
1943	Of Those Who May Not Come Back	*U. S. Coast Guard Academy Alumni Bulletin*
1946	Planning for Educational Facilities	*Vital Speeches Oct. 1946 Issue*
1946	Public Relations in Fund-Raising	*Annual Seminar, Syracuse University*
1946	Our Profession–Financing Philanthropy	*Marts & Lundy Staff Conference*
1947	Procedures for Raising Capital Funds	*Association of American Colleges Bulletin*
1947	Financing Philanthropy	*Association of American Colleges Bulletin*
1947	Every Man a Philanthropist	*Kiplinger Magazine*
1948	Historical Sketch of Fund-Raising Profession	*Marts & Lundy Staff Conference*
1948	Present Outlook for Raising Funds	*Institute of Higher Education*

BY PAUL H. YOUNGER

APPENDIX B

THE STAFF OF MARTS AND LUNDY, INCORPORATED

ARNAUD C. MARTS
Chairman of the Board

GEORGE E. LUNDY
*Honorary Chairman of the Board
and Senior Consultant*

LOUIS W. ROBEY
*Honorary Vice Chairman of the Board
and Senior Consultant*

THOMAS F. MORGAN, JR.
Senior Consultant

AUSTIN V. MCCLAIN
President

MELVIN D. BREWER
Vice President & Secretary

PAUL H. YOUNGER
Executive Vice President & Treasurer

JAMES H. DUCHINE
Vice President

HERBERT C. RICHMAN
Vice President

BOARD OF DIRECTORS

ALL OFFICERS AND

JOHN I. CARLSON
JOSEPH C. SMITH

✍

ASHLEY L. BICKMORE
TOZIER BROWN
RUSSELL G. BROWNING
WAYNE H. BURWELL
ALBERT E. CHAMBERLAIN
ERNEST B. CHAMBERLAIN
J. WILEY CHRISTIE, JR.
FRANK J. COLEMAN
RAYMOND W. COOPER
CHARLES W. CRIST
CHARLES S. DICE
HAROLD C. DUDLEY
EDWARD F. DUFFY
ROLLAND N. DUTTON
OTTO W. FERRENE
WILLIAM C. FRENCH
CHARLES H. GALE
CRAWFORD L. GILLIGAN
JOHN W. GOODNOUGH
CHARLES A. HERSCHLEB
PAUL A. HIGHTOWER

HAROLD F. HOWE
PHILIP C. KING
JOSEPH B. LECKIE
ARTHUR H. LOFGREN
GEORGE E. T. LUM
J. FLOYD MCTYIER
ARTHUR B. NICHOLLS
WILLIAM A. D. PARKS
WILLIAM LAWTON PRINCE II
SAMUEL H. RICKARD
FRANK H. ROBESON
RAYMOND F. ROPE
G. WALLACE RUCKERT
BAYARD T. SKILLING
EDWARD H. SMITH
FREDERICK W. SMITH
JOHN C. STAHLE
ARTHUR L. TAYLOR
F. PAUL TRICH
CARL H. WALKER
DOUGAL E. YOUNG

CODE OF ETHICS

MARTS & LUNDY, INC.

I. We will take no campaign the purpose of which we cannot approve.

II. We will take no campaign which in our best judgment is not possible of success.

III. We will direct no philanthropic campaigns on a percentage basis, for to do so would create the impression in the minds of the volunteer workers that our earnestness and zeal were for financial gain.

IV. Having taken a contract, the interests of the client must come before our own.

V. Our publicity shall be educational rather than of the ballyhoo or high pressure type.

VI. Directors shall at all times conduct themselves as Christian gentlemen careful to do nothing which will be likely to offend anyone.

VII. Directors shall give themselves whole-heartedly to the promotion of the campaign, utilizing every minute of every day in behalf of the campaign.

VIII. Campaigns shall be conducted upon such a high plane that there will be three results:

   1. The constituency of the institution shall become thoroughly familiar with its character, ideals and objectives;

   2. The financial objective shall be reached;

   3. Such good will for the institution shall be built that will result in great good in future years.

INDEX

DATE DUE

NOV 15 2006			
GAYLORD			PRINTED IN U.S.A.